MW01449069

WE DRIVE

Concrete Mixer Trucks

Ruby Tuesday Books

Alix Wood

Published in 2025 by Ruby Tuesday Books Ltd.

Editors: Ruth Owen & Mark J. Sachner
Design: Alix Wood
Production: John Lingham

Photo credits:
Alamy: Cover (Sharon Davis), 9 (Operation 2022), 14 (Justin Kase zsixz), 15T (Chris Mummery), 19 (Peter Righteous); Shutterstock: 1 (Drpixel), 2–3 (Bannafarsai_Stock), 4 (chuyuss), 5T (shamils/Nerthuz), 5B (Jromero04), 6T (Drpixel), 6B (Another77), 7 (grafvision), 10–11 (Vivid Brands), 11R (Henk Jacobs), 13 (Roman023_photography), 15B (andreas sunu bhakti), 16 (Roman Chekhovskoi), 17 (Dagmara_K), 18 (Rich T Photo), 20T (Aisyaqilumaranas), 20B (Unkas Photo), 21T (Ronnachaipark), 21B (BlackMac), 22T (StockMediaSeller), 22B, 23T (grafvision), 23B (Aisyaqilumaranas); Alix Wood: 8, 12.

Library of Congress Control Number: 2024948698

Print (Hardback) ISBN 978-1-78856-528-8
Print (Paperback) ISBN 978-1-78856-529-5
ePub ISBN 978-1-78856-530-1

Published in Minneapolis, MN
Printed in the United States

www.rubytuesdaybooks.com

Contents

Let's Deliver Concrete!

These buildings, bridges, and roads are all made from **concrete**.

Concrete is a mixture of cement, water, sand, and gravel or crushed rock.

Cement

Water

Gravel

Sand

How did all the concrete get there?

Drivers delivered it in big concrete mixer trucks.

A driver arrives early at the **concrete plant.**

He fills the truck's water tank with a hose.

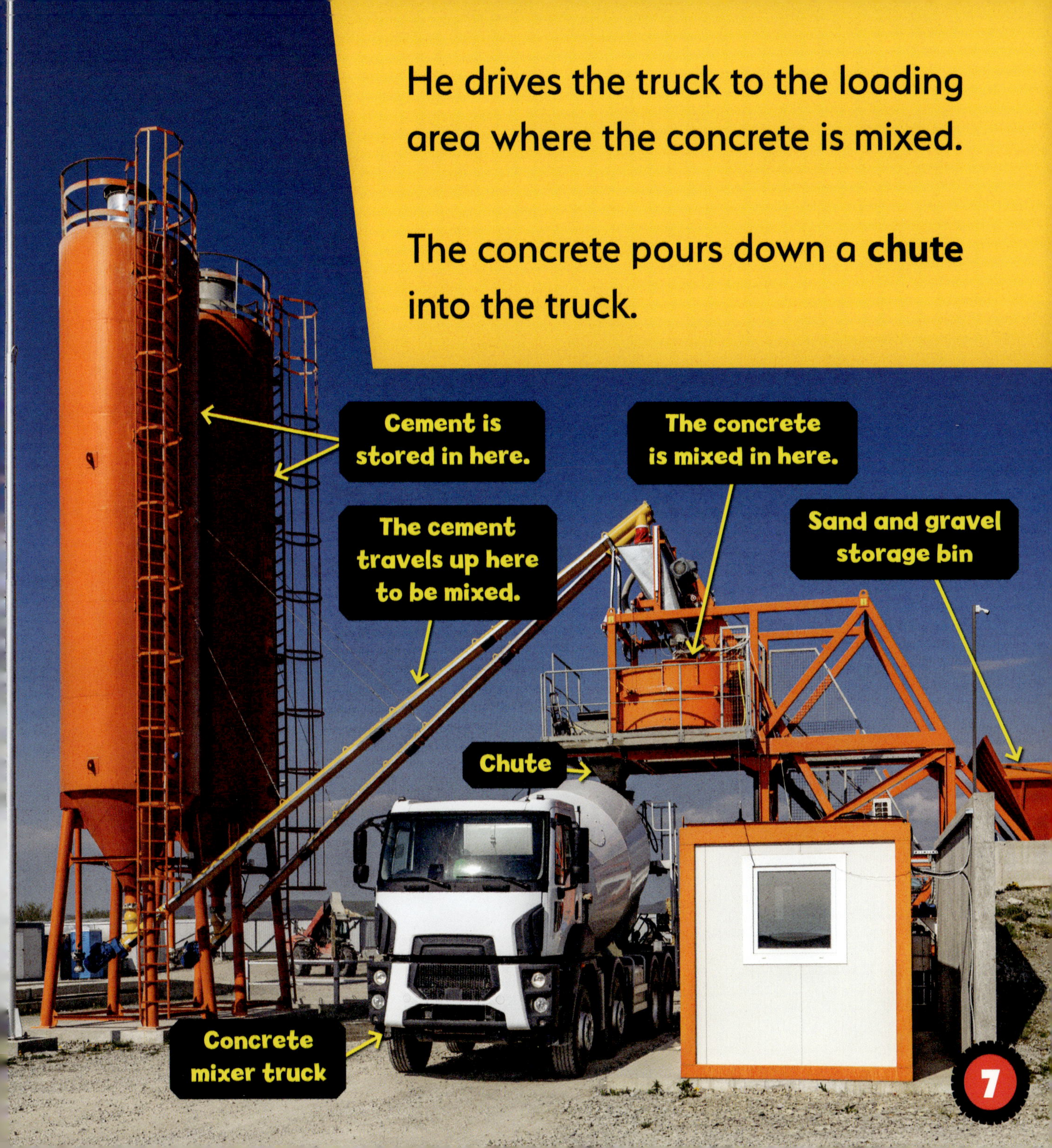
He drives the truck to the loading area where the concrete is mixed.
The concrete pours down a **chute** into the truck.
Cement is stored in here.
The concrete is mixed in here.
The cement travels up here to be mixed.
Sand and gravel storage bin
Chute
Concrete mixer truck

Concrete starts to harden once the cement is mixed with water.

A spiral blade inside the drum turns and mixes the concrete to keep it from getting hard.

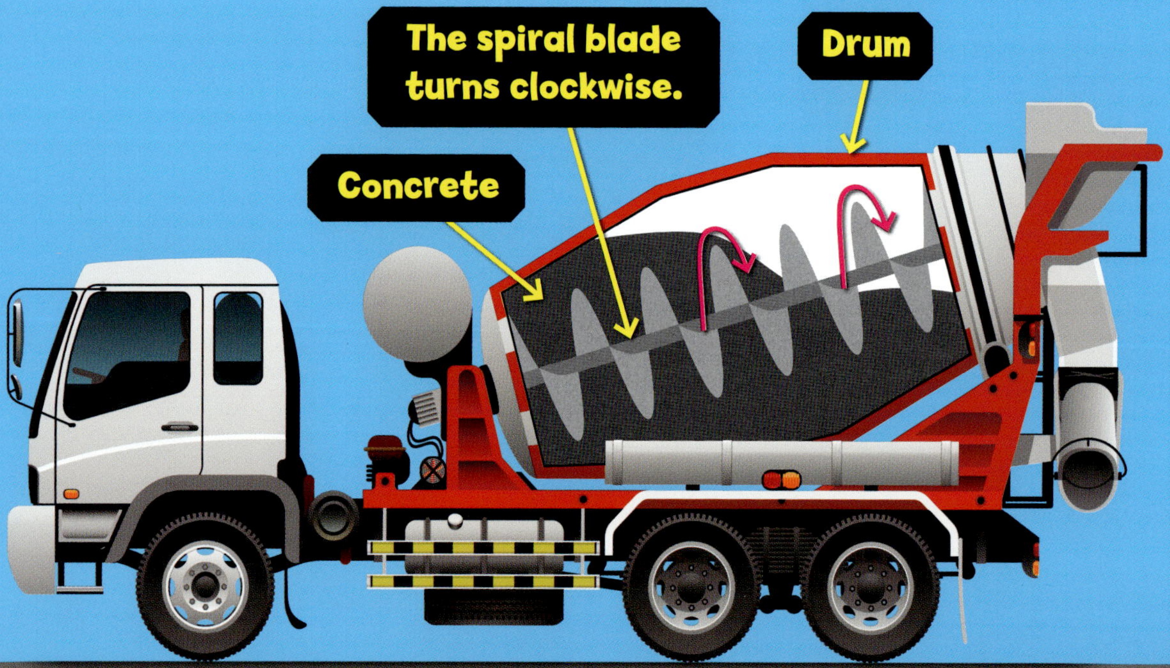

However, concrete spoils if it is mixed for too long.

The driver must get to the construction site quickly.

Construction workers will check the mix—it must be not too wet and not too dry.

Testing the mix

The driver uses a remote control to make the drum's blade turn counterclockwise.

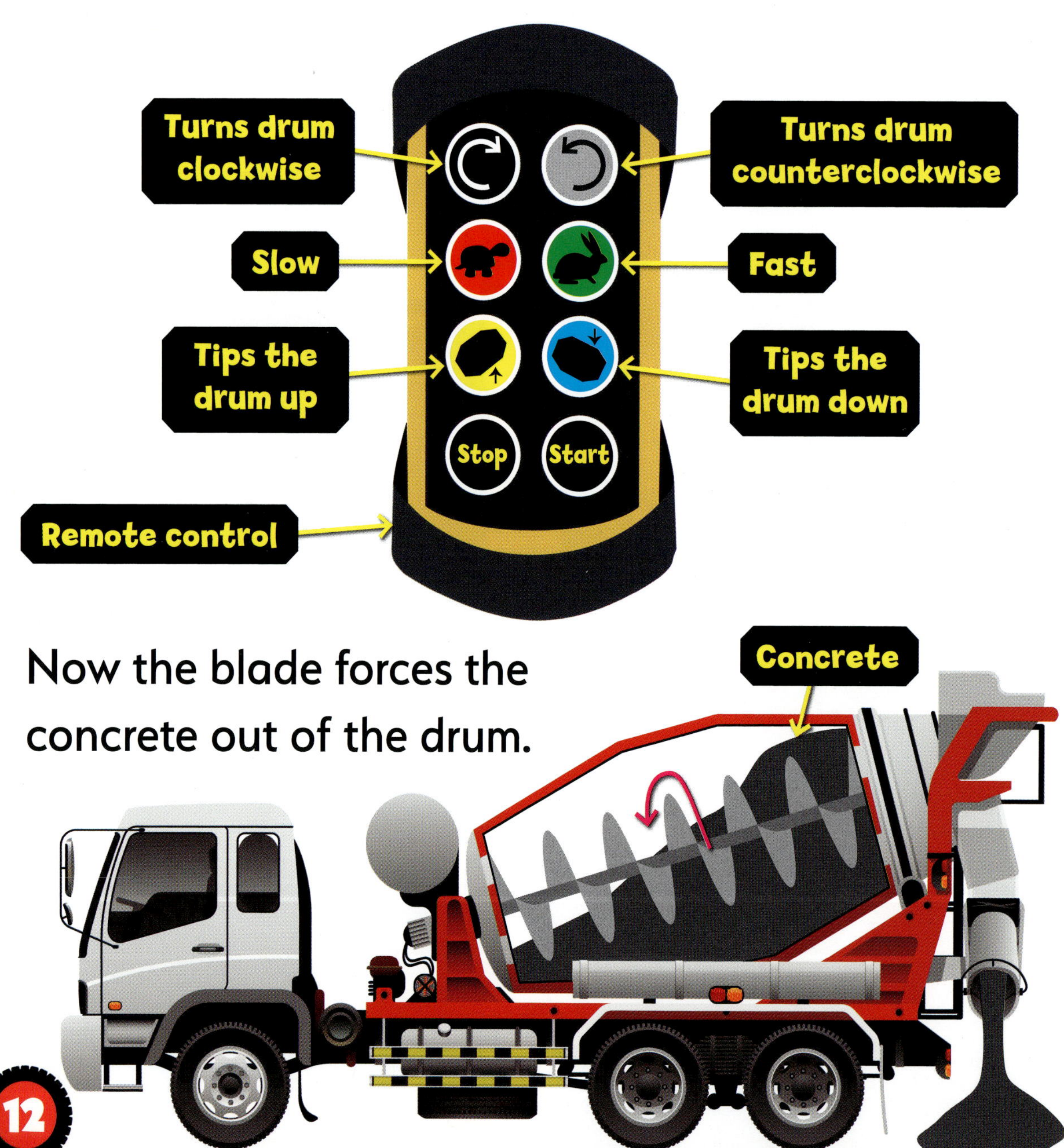

Now the blade forces the concrete out of the drum.

The concrete pours into a **mold** the construction workers have made.

The concrete in the mold dries and makes a strong, hard block.

Now the truck must be cleaned quickly before any leftover concrete sets hard.

The driver hoses the outside of the truck and squirts water into the drum.

Back at the plant, the driver cleans the inside of the drum.

A clean drum

The leftover concrete can be recycled into new concrete once it dries.

Concrete mixers can't always park where the concrete is needed.

Then the concrete is pumped into a long hose.

A robotic arm moves the hose to where it is needed.

A pump operator moves the hose to spread the concrete.

The hose can be hard to control!

A worker might unload the concrete by wheelbarrow.

It's hard work—each barrow weighs the same as a heavy man!

Construction workers might use wheelbarrows to lay a concrete floor.

Drivers need to look after the concrete, so they don't help push the wheelbarrows.

This driver is pouring concrete into a bucket attached to a crane.

The crane lifts the concrete up to where it is needed.

At the end of the day the drivers head back to the plant.

They proudly pass the buildings they help make.

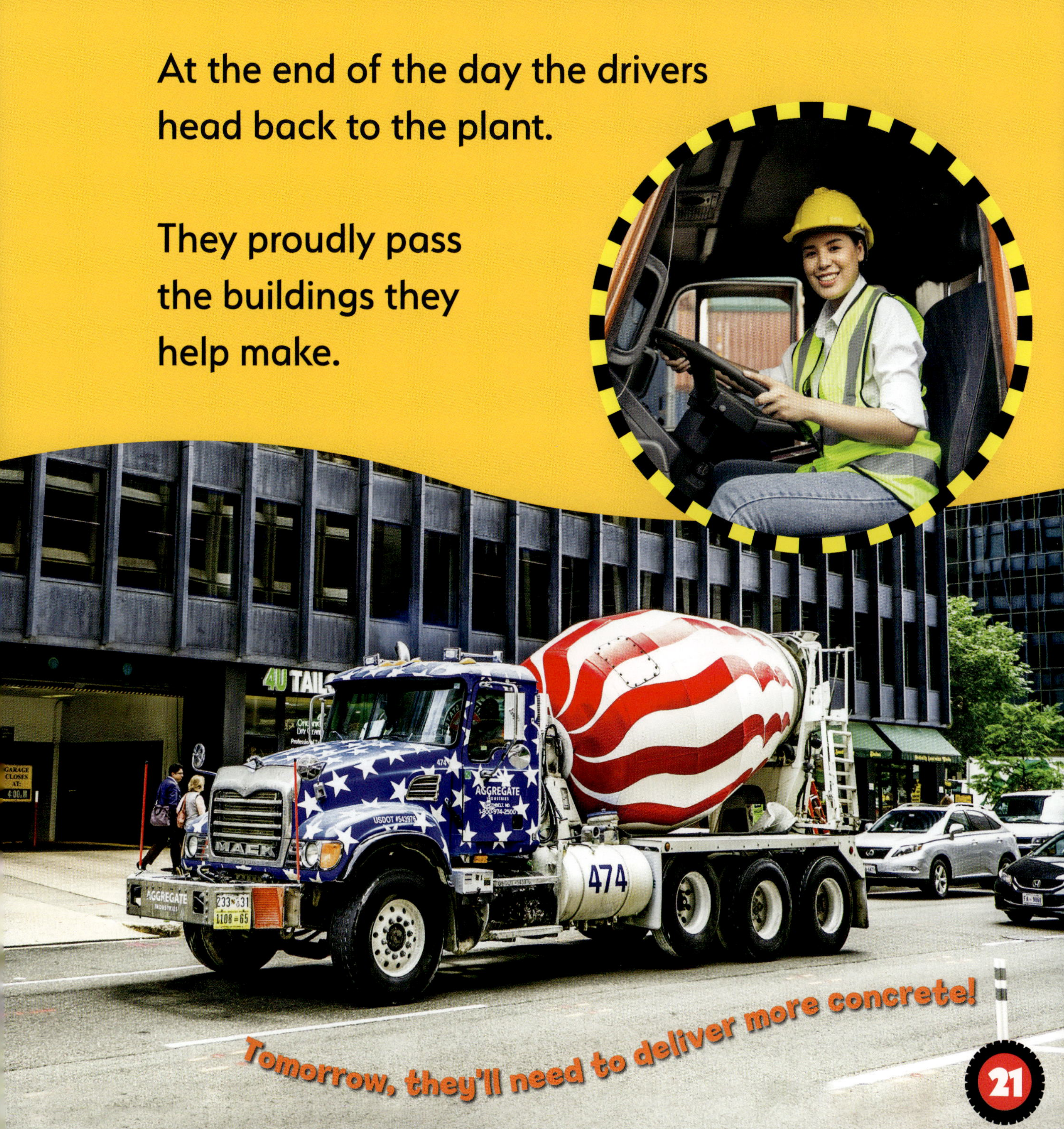

Tomorrow, they'll need to deliver more concrete!

Glossary

chute
A passage down which things can slide in order to move from one place to another.

concrete
A hard construction material made from a mixture of broken stone or gravel, sand, cement, and water.

concrete plant
A place that stores and mixes the materials that are used to make concrete.

mold
A hollow container that is used to shape a soft or liquid substance that is poured into it.

Index